MW00965356

Nature's Window

ELEPHANTS

Nature's Window

ELEPHANTS

Sheila Buff

**Andrews McMeel
Publishing**

Kansas City

I NTRODUCTION

Elephants are big. That's a bold statement, but easily backed up by the numbers: The average elephant, well over ten feet tall, weighs about twelve thousand pounds. With long trunks, massive tusks, and sheer size, elephants are both distinctive and formidable. Even so, these smart animals are basically gentle, attacking only when threatened.

Elephants share some characteristics

Elephants are second only to whales as the largest animals in the world. At birth, an elephant weighs nearly three hundred pounds; by adulthood, it will weigh well over ten thousand pounds.

with humans. Like us, they live in stable family groups, with highly dependent young. They are also long-lived (surviving up to the age of seventy), highly intelligent, and communicative, easily keeping track of each other over large areas.

We have long attributed mythical and spiritual qualities to elephants. The Hindu deity Ganesh, god of wisdom, is represented by an elephant with a broken tusk. In Thailand, elephants are earthly representatives of mythical winged elephants, who in turn represent Buddha. In African folklore, elephants are portrayed as wise and powerful.

In more practical terms, elephants have an important economic role in human lives. In India, Thailand, and parts of southeast Asia, elephants have worked as beasts of burden for centuries, particularly in tropical logging operations, and are also used ceremonially, in religious processions.

UNDERSTANDING ELEPHANTS

Elephants belong to the group of animals called proboscideans, or trunk bearers, that evolved some fifty-five million years ago. Today only two species survive, the African elephant, found across the grasslands and forests of the entire sub-Saharan region, and the Asian elephant, which roams the forested regions of southeast Asia.

Young elephants can pick up food and other things with their flexible trunks when they are just a few months old. By the time this juvenile is an adult, its trunk will be eight feet long.

The two elephant species differ in important ways. The African elephant, which is larger than the Asian elephant, has a straight back and

very large ears. The tip of the trunk has two "fingers," one each on the upper and lower sides. Both male and female African elephants have tusks, which are actually very elongated upper incisor teeth. The tusks start to appear when an elephant is about two years old and grow throughout its lifetime. The longest tusk on record is ten feet long and weighs nearly 230 pounds.

Asian elephants are noticeably smaller than their African counterparts and have domed heads, rounded backs, and small, round

An elephant's tusks grow throughout its life and can easily reach lengths of eight feet or more. Elephants are left- or right-tusked. The tusk they use more often gets worn down faster.

ears. A large adult male weighs five to six tons and stands ten feet tall at the shoulder; female Asian elephants weigh about half as much as males. The tip of the trunk has just one "finger" on the upper side, while the bottom is a sort of thick pad. Only male Asian elephants have long tusks—females have much shorter tusks called tushes. Interestingly, because of a genetic quirk, most of the Asian elephants found on the island of Sri Lanka have no tusks at all, regardless of sex.

Asian elephants have much smaller, more rounded ears than African elephants. Individual elephants can be identified by the vein pattern and the various tears, holes, and other marks on their ears.

THE ELEPHANT HERD

Elephants are highly social animals. In general, they live in small, closely knit groups of between six and twelve animals, although larger herds of twelve to twenty are quite common. The leader of a herd, or its matriarch, is an older female, often more than forty years old. Herd members are her daughters and their young male and female offspring, along with some of the matriarch's sisters, nieces, and grandnieces.

When a bull (male) elephant reaches his

Elephants walking in a herd raise a lot of dust but make surprisingly little noise as they move on huge, thickly padded feet. A walking elephant can travel at about five miles per hour for hours on end.

An elephant herd usually has about ten closely related members, ranging in age from newborn to sixty years. Sometimes smaller herds come together briefly, perhaps because they contain related females, and then split apart again.

teenage years and becomes sexually mature, he breaks away from the herd. From that time, he wanders on his own, or sometimes joins together with a few other young males in a bachelor herd. Older, more mature bulls (past the age of thirty) are basically solitary. Males seek out the herd only to mate with a receptive female and have nothing to do with raising the young.

The herd depends heavily on the knowledge and experience of the leader. During periods of drought, for example, the matriarch may be the only elephant in the herd who remembers the location of a distant water hole. She knows where the richest food sources are and how to avoid hazards. The matriarch leads the herd in times of danger, deciding whether to threaten, attack, or retreat.

Members of the herd act together to protect their young. When threatened, the herd forms a circle facing outward. The young elephants crowd into the center or stand beneath their mothers. The sight and sound of a herd of angry, trumpeting elephants usually frightens off predators such as lions, tigers, and wild dogs.

ELEPHANT LIFE CYCLE

On average, elephants live sixty-five years. Among mammals, only humans live as long. And like humans, elephants have a long childhood and adolescence.

A newborn elephant calf may be big, but it's still a baby. An average calf weighs about 260 pounds and stands just under three feet tall—exactly the right height to fit under its mother's belly. All the members of the herd help care for the calf.

A female reaches sexual maturity when she

Elephants have thick skin, but it is surprisingly sensitive to sun, parasites, and biting insects. Frequent mud or dust baths help to provide a protective coating.

is about twelve years old, even though she isn't fully grown. Males reach full maturity later, in their twenties.

Every two years or so, a mature female elephant has a breeding period, called estrus, when she is sexually receptive. Male elephants can scent a receptive female's odor from miles away; they may also hear her subsonic calls. Several males may come courting the same female, but only the most dominant will mate with her.

Healthy bull elephants in their mating years regularly enter into musth—a state of heightened sexuality that can last several weeks or more—once or twice a year. The bull's level of the male hormone testosterone skyrockets during musth. The word musth comes from a Sanskrit word meaning intoxicated. It's an apt description; a bull in musth is very aggressive and irritable.

Pregnancy in the Asian elephant lasts between eighteen and twenty-two months, though male babies may take even longer to gestate. Pregnancy in the African elephant isn't as well understood, but may last longer. Because of the long gestation and dependency period, a

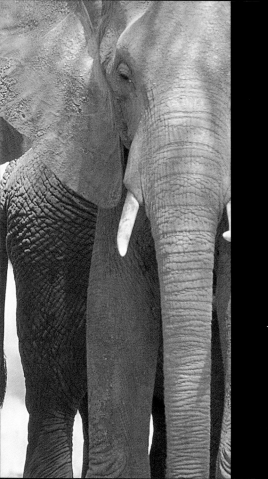

Under the leadership of the matriarch, a formidable wall of elephants stands flank to flank and faces outward against a possible threat. Young and baby elephants huddle for protection behind the adults.

female gives birth only about once every four to five years. She'll continue to have calves until she is about fifty.

Once an elephant reaches old age, its teeth become so worn that it cannot eat properly and soon dies. Members of a herd seem to understand and mourn another's death. They will cover the body with branches and grass and may remain disconsolately in the area for days. Returning to the site years later, they seem to recognize the bones they find and associate them with the lost member.

Like a human, this Asian elephant's brain and body will develop fully during a long childhood and adolescence. Full adulthood begins around the age of twenty and lasts for several decades.

ELEPHANTS EATING

Elephants are vegetarians, eating almost anything that grows. It takes a lot of vegetation—between 250 and 500 pounds a day—to feed an adult. To gather that much food, an elephant spends at least sixteen hours a day foraging and eating. It may take a break from feeding and rest for an hour or so during the hottest part of the day, but it sleeps (always standing up) for only four hours each night.

An elephant uses its long, flexible trunk to

An elephant's trunk has no bones: Flexibility comes from nearly 150,000 muscles and an array of nerves. African elephants use their two "fingers" to grasp food, much as humans pinch with fingers.

seize food and bring it to its mouth. The trunk, actually an extension of the nose and upper lip, is about eight feet long and weighs up to three hundred pounds. Elephants also use their trunks to rip large branches off trees, strip bark from trees, or even to knock trees over to reach succulent leaves and fruit. This may seem destructive, but in fact, it plays an important ecological role by opening up clearings and allowing grasses and other vegetation to take root and grow.

An elephant's four, ridged molars (each twelve inches

long) are well adapted for crushing and grinding coarse plant foods, including grasses, leaves, fruits, and tree bark.

In addition to consuming large amounts of food, elephants need a lot of water. An African elephant can drink more than fifty gallons in just a few minutes; each trunkful alone can hold over two gallons. In times of drought, elephants use their tusks and trunks to dig down below the surface of lakes and stream beds to find hidden supplies. While satisfying their own water needs, they open up a water source for other animals as well.

ELEPHANT COMMUNICATION

For centuries, humans were mystified by the way elephants seemed to communicate silently with each other over long distances. When elephants in a herd spread out widely to feed, for example, they always seemed to know where all the others were. They also seemed to know exactly where other herds were, even when the other animals were miles away. Solitary bull elephants could locate female herds from great distances. After watching an elephant stand still and flap

When they're close, elephants communicate with a variety of roars, squeals, and other noises. To communicate over long distances, they use subsonic rumbles, which are inaudible to humans.

its ears, and then lift its head and spread its ears as if listening, many an observer became convinced that elephants possessed telepathic abilities.

In 1984, researcher Katharine Payne discovered that elephants communicate using infrasound—sound waves that are subsonic, or below the threshold of human hearing. Infrasound travels long distances and can be heard by elephants up to six miles away. Elephants in a grazing herd, spread out over several miles, keep track of each other with frequent infrasound contact calls. Elephants use infrasound and other calls to keep in touch in heavily forested areas, where they can't see each other. Although humans can't hear it, infrasound comes in very loud and clear to elephant ears. Some of the individual rumbles go on for up to six seconds; an elephant might continue vocalizing for ten minutes at a time.

Aside from the subsonic rumblings, elephants make a surprising number of other noises that humans *can* hear. The most familiar is the loud trumpet of an aggressive elephant. Other sounds range from roars and rumbles to

Touching each other with trunks is an important part of elephant communication. Elephants sometimes greet each other with a "trunk shake," twining their trunks together. They may also place the tip of the trunk into another elephant's mouth or drape their trunk over another's.

screams and high-pitched squeals. In all, Payne and other researchers have identified more than thirty-five elephant noises that seem to have distinctly different meanings. Some even may be meant to identify individuals, as if the elephants have named each other.

Another important aspect of elephant communication is touch. Elephants frequently rub up to each other, lean together, or stand in a huddle. Young elephants often lean against their mother. The contact reinforces the strong group bond and reassures the animals.

Elephants caress and sniff each other frequently with their trunks. When two elephants meet, they may twine their trunks together in a "trunk shake." Much like a human handshake, the trunk twining communicates friendship and affection. When two young males meet, a trunk shake can turn into a playful wrestling match.

Communication keeps the herd cohesive. When members of a herd are reunited after a separation, for example, they greet each other with rumbles, trumpeting, trunk twining, and joyful ear-flapping.

CONSERVATION

The ancient Greeks first used the word *elephas* some six thousand years ago to mean ivory, a mysterious and very valuable substance that came from faraway India. It wasn't until Alexander the Great saw living elephants in India in the fourth century B.C. that the connection between ivory and elephant tusks was made.

That connection has led to the steady destruction of the elephant for its ivory. The slaughter continued for centuries, but in the

A mahout (trainer) rides his elephant at a logging camp in Thailand. An Asian elephant in harness can drag loads weighing several thousand pounds without causing environmental damage.

last half of this century it has accelerated rapidly, driven by soaring ivory prices, powerful firearms, and lax policing. The illegal slaughter of elephants in Africa reached a tragic peak in the 1980s, when some 700,000 elephants were killed by poachers. In Tanzania's famed Serengeti National Park, the number of elephants dropped from 3,000 to 450 in just six years.

In India and other countries, domesticated elephants play important roles in ceremonial processions. This elephant in Jaipur, India, is adorned with harmless painted decorations.

The situation was somewhat better in India and other countries of southeast Asia, where a tradition of respect for elephants led to less

A large herd of African elephants marches off into the savannah. As human populations in Africa and Asia grow and people and elephants come into increasing competition and conflict, sights like this may become very rare.

poaching. Even so, only 18,000 to 24,000 elephants remain in the wild in India today, and just 37,000 to 57,000 remain wild in all of Asia, along with some 16,000 in captivity.

In 1989, a worldwide ban on the international ivory trade was finally enacted. Combined with improved enforcement, the ban has slowed the slaughter considerably. The future for these gentle giants looks brighter than it once did, but it is far from secure.

Over the past century, the world's elephants were illegally slaughtered to near extinction for their valuable tusks. Today elephants are protected by a worldwide ban on the ivory trade.

Photography credits

All images provided by ENP Images except page 43.

© Gerry Ellis: pages 2, 4, 9, 10, 13, 15, 16–17, 20, 24–25, 27, 29, 32, 36–37, 40, 47;

© Robert Holmes: page 43; © Pete Oxford: pages 44–45;

Front jacket: © Gerry Ellis;

Back jacket: © Gerry Ellis

www.andrewsmcmeel.com

ISBN: 0-8362-5327-2

Printed in Singapore

First U.S. edition

1 3 5 7 9 10 8 6 4 2

Editor: Deri Reed
Art Director: Tomek Lamprecht
Designer: Paola Pelosi

Produced by Smallwood & Stewart, Inc., New York City